CW01305533

It's All About Grace

* * *

*A story of God's grace,
His love and provision in a time of crisis.*

© IAAG Publishing 2024

Contents

Chapter 1: Chicago   10

Chapter 2: An Encounter with God   14

Chapter 3: A Country Divided   28

Chapter 4: Our Marriage   38

Chapter 5: Coincidences?   44

Chapter 6: Miracle(s)   58

Chapter 7: A New Home   72

Epilogue   84

It's all About Grace

Dedication

* * *

To my dear husband, David, and my parents, Claudius, and Isabella Major, who prayed and cared for all the family whilst Grace and I went to Chicago for treatment.

'For it is by God's grace that you have been saved through faith. It is not the result of your own efforts, but God's gift, so no one can boast about it.'

- Ephesians 2:8-9

Foreword

I used to think that my mother was a peculiar woman. She didn't seem like anyone I knew growing up. We lived in a small town in the middle of England called Sutton Coldfield, several miles north of Birmingham. For as long as I can remember, she seemed to possess an otherworldly sense of things. She could predict people's behaviour, see events unfolding years before they happened, and held what seemed to me then a strange belief in God. I say strange because that's the most apt description I can give it.

At times, I thought she was crazy, but that's where the contradiction in my mind occurred: she couldn't possibly be crazy. She was an educated woman, a doctor no less—a scientist. She was the smartest person I knew. I watched my teachers squirm and completely change their demeanour during parents' evenings when she discussed my education with them; they were out of their depth.

Most parents I knew at the time, didn't remember in great detail the subjects they learned in school - unless they were related to their jobs. Yet, my mum taught me maths, recited poetry, and excelled in science. So, you can imagine my bewilderment and concern about how this academically accomplished, reasonable, and logical woman believed in some unknowable, invisible entity we call 'God' and claimed to have a relationship with 'it'.

But as I grew up and got to know her better (I always think that's a strange thing to say—you know, 'getting to know your parents'—but I suppose you do), it became clearer that she wasn't peculiar at all. In fact, she was still the most logical and rational person I knew.

My mother is a doctor. She was trained to observe and listen, to analyse and deduce the most likely answer to any question she faced. So, when you encounter a litany of coincidences that seem to be precisely, and I mean precisely, what was 'prayed' for or some strange miraculous occurrence on an almost daily basis, it undoubtedly colours the way you see the world.

I mention again that my mother is a doctor, not to brag, but to reinforce a fairly unanimous sentiment among anyone who knows her: her modus operandi is to help people. She was the first person who taught me about 'caring' for others. She placed huge emphasis on not tolerating anything that resembled selfish behaviour. For as long as I can remember, she has opened her home and heart to anyone and everyone.

We always had many people in our home at any given time. Before my sisters and I were born, she and Dad already had a full house of children, with at least two of my older cousins living with them in Liberia. As my sisters and I left the family home for university or adulthood, Mum would have exchange students or someone she knew living in the house.

At Christmas, while most were opening their presents at home—a time children look forward to because of the gifts—Mum and Dad ensured we never forgot the meaning of Christmas in a very practical way. We often had our Christmas day meal at our local church, which put on a meal for those in the community who would be alone during Christmas time.

A running joke in our family is that Mum was already an adult as a child because she was so sensible. It was like she was incapable of mistakes, which she obviously wasn't, but the point is that she always thought of the best, most loving, and caring option. To her, it made logical sense as it was the option that benefited the most people.

This short summary of my experience with my mum is why I believe she wrote this book. Her entire life has been dedicated to helping anyone and everyone she can. She will always choose to uplift, share an anecdote, pray with, support, and encourage everyone she encounters.

This book captures a little of why my mum is who she is. She has been immeasurably blessed during her lifetime, and as a result, she's chosen to share and facilitate God's blessings to others.

The story of my sister, Grace, as told by my mum in this book, is one that I hope will encourage and inspire you today to have a little faith. You never know where it will take you.

- A. Archibald Troko

Acknowledgements

What an incredible story of how Velma has kept and still is keeping her eyes on God, the Author and Finisher of her faith. The Lord has enabled her to tell a long and complicated story in a very uncomplicated way, spanning years and so many milestones of your life.

Truly the central theme shouts out loudly and clearly: "It's all about Grace, God's amazing grace. Thank you for being obedient to the call of God to write this book; to honour your husband and honour God. A wonderful book and very inspiring to read.

- Mrs. Connie (Yhap) Brown, New Jersey, USA

Velma's graduation day from medical school in Liberia in 1980

Chapter 1:
Chicago

It's all About Grace

In the heart of Chicago, I found myself seated in solitude beneath the harsh glow of fluorescent lights within the hospital's lobby. The night had draped its stillness over everything. The expanse of the room encircled me, deserted, whilst the outside sky loomed in darkness through the windows.

The coffee kiosk and shops sat closed and shuttered. For over an hour, the only person I saw was a cleaner, who occasionally wandered in with a mop or broom. The air had that typical hospital smell – antiseptic, a little bitter, with undertones of bleach and soap. It was a smell that I had become very used to over the years.

I spent that hour doing the same thing I had been doing for most of the last month, praying, but this time, the prayers had a new intensity. Despite my belief and trust in God, it was natural for me, as a mother, to panic. My little girl, my precious three-year-old daughter, Grace, lay unconscious upstairs in the operating theatre, her skull open, her brain exposed, as doctors tried to save her life.

Every now and again, I stood, pacing back and forth, then settled again to offer more prayers.

Whist I was physically alone, I knew God was with me. At times like this, you need faith. Without it, I don't know how I would have coped.

'Dear God, please protect and watch over Grace. You gave her to us, and I don't think you are going to let her go now.'

Earlier, in the evening, I had called my husband David, who was more than 5,000 miles away in Monrovia, Liberia.

'Darling,' I said, 'the CT scan has shown an abscess in the back of her brain, and the surgeon doesn't want to wait another night. They are doing the surgery tonight. Time is of the essence. You all need to be praying too.'

'What?!?', David's voice was panicked and then silence. 'Are you there?' I asked. 'Yes', he said softly. 'I'll tell everyone – all our family and friends. I'll ask them all to pray for Grace.'

By that time, our praying Christian community, had become international and encompassed hundreds of people.

What great strength that gave me! As I paced and sat, paced, and sat, there was not a moment when I despaired.

With all the ways in which God had guided us throughout the years and the series of events that had brought us here for the surgery, I knew the Almighty was looking out for us.

I knew the accumulated power of all that prayer would create a tidal wave of holy power. I knew he had a plan for us, but, when I saw the surgeon walking towards me through the open doors, my heart thundered in my chest. My breath caught in my throat.

As the man who held my daughter's fate in his hands opened his mouth to speak, I resolved to welcome whatever would come. God's love was all that mattered. And I trusted it completely. After all, God had been with me for my whole life.

Whoever goes to the Lord for safety, remains under the protection of the LORD.

- Psalm 91:1

It's all About Grace

David and Velma at John and Elaine Stob's house in Chicago, 1986

David Van Reken, SIM Missionary and Paediatrician, who facilitated Grace's treatment in 1986.

Chapter 2:
An Encounter with God

My early years were spent in Sinoe County before my family moved to Monrovia, Liberia's capital city, a bustling metropolis of half a million people. I lived there with my parents, brothers, and sisters in a typical large and happy Liberian family. I was the second eldest daughter, although I had two older siblings who sadly passed away. My parents were warm and supportive, my father worked for the Government and was appointed Superintendent of our county. My mother worked as a Primary School teacher and later, a Continuing Education Teacher in an Afternoon School.

As was common in West Africa, religion was a big part of our lives, and we were raised as Christians. Both my parents were proud Methodists and went to church often. Spirituality was woven into the cultural fabric of Liberia, and nearly everybody I knew was either a Christian or had some form of religious affiliation.

Although I was raised as a Christian and attended a Christian high school in Monrovia, ultimately, as a young woman, I made my own decision to follow Jesus. All the way through school, I participated in every faith-based activity and was a committed member of the church. In that sense, I thought of myself as a Christian from an early age. After all, I followed all the rules and practised as others did. What I did not know at that stage, what I *could* not know until it happened, was that I was yet to come to my own reckoning with God.

I did well in all my studies and graduated in first place in my high school class in 1970 I then went on to study at the University of Liberia in Monrovia majoring in Chemistry and Biology. While pursuing my studies, I remained a believer, although I went to church less often as a student, maybe every few weeks. Then, in 1973, at the end of the third year of my four-year degree programme, I began to seriously think about my life and future. Major existential questions played in my mind. What was the point of being in this world? What was my purpose? What was I trying to achieve? I suspect everyone has a moment like this at some point. It was not a personal crisis but a time of asking, *'Why?'*

Following the practices of my upbringing, I decided that the best thing to do was to ask God. He would guide me. So, I started to pray about it.

'God, why am I feeling like this?' I asked. 'I'm finishing university soon and feel I need direction.'

Searching for input, I began attending church every week again, as I had as a young girl. Still, the answer that I needed evaded me. Then, one came at a time when I was least expecting it. God, I was to discover, often works this way. You cannot predict when or how His intervention will come.

At that time, between 1971 and 1974, I used to have long chemistry lab sessions, usually about four hours, two or three afternoons a week. It was quite tiring, so I adopted the habit of taking a siesta after lunch on those days before going to the laboratory.

On one of those occasions, as I lay on my bed in my room, I was woken up by a voice.

'Velma,' the voice said. 'You need to commit your life to Jesus.'

I sat up as if I had been electrified and looked left and right. Where had the voice come from? My first thought was that there was somebody outside the door. I crossed the room, opened the door, and looked outside. Of course, no one was there. I looked out of the window. Again, there was no one around.

Immediately, I sank to my knees on the floor and clasped my hands in prayer.

'God,' I said. 'I don't know what is happening to me. But whatever you say. If I must commit my life to Jesus, then I'm going to do that.'

My grandmother had given me a Bible as a present when I graduated from high school. It had a beautiful white cover, and I kept it in a box on a shelf above my bed. This felt like the time to take it from its box. I gently lifted it out and began to read passages. Suddenly, lots of things seemed to make sense.

At the university, there was a Christian fellowship that met every morning before the day's studies. I decided to start attending these prayer meetings, even though I was not an early riser. The meetings convened at 7.30 a.m., and I did not set an alarm, but after hearing that voice, something inside me had *changed*. Now that I had made a personal commitment, I woke every morning for the prayer fellowship without a problem. I felt my faith blooming inside me like a flower, and through my membership in that fellowship, I was invited to a PAFES (Pan-African Fellowship of Evangelical Students) Conference for Christian students at Njala University, Sierra Leone, West Africa in July 1973.

There are many historical connections between Liberia and Sierra Leone, which meant they collaborated on many joint projects. On this occasion, Sierra Leone, was hosting the PAFES Conference for university students from Liberia and Sierra Leone. I looked forward to the conference very much and couldn't wait to attend.

All my travel documents were prepared, but the journey was due to take place by bus during the rainy season. During this time of year, many of the unpaved, mud roads of the country became unpassable, and there were doubts about whether the university minibus would get us there safely. My father, in particular, was extremely concerned.

'It is not a sensible time to travel by road.' He shook his head.

My mother took a different approach. 'Oh, come on. Velma left us so many years ago,' she said, 'to go to boarding school and then university, and you're worrying about something like this? The same God who has been looking after her since she left here is going to look after her now. In fact, she's going to a Christian conference, for God's sake! There's no way He will allow her to come to any harm.'

With my father's doubts vanquished by my mother's faith, I prepared for the trip, excited about what I would experience.

We had been given a list of books to read prior to the conference. There was one called *In His Steps* by Charles Sheldon, which a lot of discussion would be based around and seemed fairly essential. The day before I was due to travel, I went to a Christian bookshop to get a copy, and while I was there, I met one of the leaders of the University Christian Fellowship. I asked her what time we were leaving the next day.

'What? We didn't know you were still coming,' she said. 'We thought you had changed your mind.'

'What do you mean?' I cried. 'I have done all the paperwork.'

'We heard that you were talking it over with your parents and your father did not want you to go. So, we didn't put your name on the final list of delegates to be sent to the embassy.'

'No!' I said. 'This is a mistake. I am supposed to be going.'

The fellowship leader could see I was upset, so we left the store together, and outside in the street, we asked God for guidance on what to do. We decided to go to the foreign ministry in Monrovia to see if I could obtain a travel permit on short notice, and so we ran. It was a short distance, but we ran all the way from the Christian bookshop to the foreign ministry.

Once there, breathless, and sweaty, we found the travel permit office, where the official on duty was just closing. We had arrived just in time and explained the situation in anxious voices.

'Do you know?' the man said, smiling. 'God must really want you to go on this journey. I was supposed to leave this office 30 minutes ago, but for some reason, I stayed.

I don't know why. I didn't really even have anything to do. It's like something strange was keeping me here.' He paused, with a reflective expression. 'We have already sent the papers to the Sierra Leone embassy,' he said. 'But maybe there is still a way to make it work.'

Once again, I found myself amazed and grateful as the official prepared the *Laissez-passer* for me, attached my documents to it and stamped it. He said I would be able to use this as proof of my permission to travel if anybody asked. As a result of that series of events, I found myself on the bus to Sierra Leone the next morning. The eight-hour journey passed without a problem, and I arrived in a positive frame of mind.

The conference was a wonderful experience in many ways. I especially enjoyed being surrounded by like-minded people of a similar age to me. Several days passed of fascinating speakers and discussions, all very uplifting, when something began to stir inside me. Something I hadn't known before. A joy, a love, and a longing for more. Everything about God suddenly made complete sense.

The teaching for the week, was based on Paul's letter to the Ephesians, the first book written in the New Testament. Brother Dankwa, or 'TB', as he was affectionately called, taught from this book, line by line. It was about how we have been chosen by God, based on his grace and not conditional on *anything* we could do.

During the middle of the week, I attended an evening session during which I had an experience. It seemed that my ears and eyes were suddenly opened, and I understood the love of God. It was overwhelming and embracing.

As I sat in the middle of the room, I simply began to cry. The tears flowed down my cheeks as if my spirit had been transferred somewhere else. In my imagination, I could *see* the love of God. I could *actually* visualise it. Everything was contained in it – compassion, forgiveness and infinite joy and devotion. That's why Jesus died, I realised. There was nothing I had to carry, no burden. It was all taken care of. When I left the meeting that evening, still in tears, I approached the speaker.

'I don't know what happened to me!' I told him. 'God's love is just so overwhelming.'

'Yes,' he said simply. 'I know; I know.'

For it is by God's grace that you have been saved through faith. It is not the result of your own efforts…

- Ephesian 2:8 & 9

We prayed together before I left, and when I went outside into the village of Bo, where the university campus was located, and began to walk back to my lodgings, the world looked different. Everything seemed bright and shiny. Even though it was night-time, if I looked down, I could see individual blades of grass, as if my vision had been enhanced.

The next day, the grass looked greener. The sky looked bluer. People looked different. I felt as though I just wanted to give everyone a hug. Something had changed inside me, and I knew it was because I had been suffused with the love of God.

Within a few days, we left the conference and returned to Liberia, and from there, my life took on a completely different focus. I told my friends what had happened to me in Sierra Leone. Most of them looked at me with incredulity. At the time, I had a boyfriend. I said to him,

'Oh, my life has changed!'

'Velma, for goodness' sake,' he replied. 'Come on, we're all Christians.'

'I know,' I told him. 'But it's different for me now.'

It was difficult to make him understand, but as far as I was concerned, it was like I had been *born again*.

Over the coming months, my life became different. I put much more emphasis on church and Bible study. Those things became a priority. It meant my friendship group shifted. Some old friends who did not share my new commitment drifted away from me, while I made new friends who joined me on my spiritual path. I broke up with my boyfriend, although we remained friends. We simply were not walking the same road.

Walking with God

After completing my four-year degree, I found myself faced with another decision. Attending medical school had always been something that I had considered, but now that the moment was upon me, I was not sure. Again, I felt the need for guidance.

'I will only go to medical school if that is what God wants me to do,' I said to myself.

As soon as my studies were over, I devoted myself to prayer. I spent two weeks just praying and praying and praying, almost as if I was on a retreat. I did not leave my house.

I felt I needed a signal and asked God to make it clear that his plan was for me to go into medicine. As a result of this, I did not apply to the medical school before the deadline. I did not want to force through an application until I understood God's intentions.

My aunt, whom I was staying with, noticed that I had not done much since leaving university and became concerned. She came to see me in my room.

'Come on, what are you going to do now?' she asked.

'I'm waiting for God to open the door and show me what I need to do,' I explained.

'I see,' she said. 'Well, there's somebody here to see you.'

'Who?'

'I don't know who he is, but he has asked to see you. He says he's from the medical school.'

'What?!' I replied.

Why on earth would someone from the medical school come to my aunt's house? I went downstairs to find a man that I had never seen before, seated in the living room.

'Excuse me,' he said. 'Velma Major?'

I nodded.

'You don't know me, but I am one of the administrators at the medical school. I am a registrar there.'

'I see,' I said, finding this all very strange.

'We have been trying to contact you because we had information from the university that you were interested in joining us, but we haven't received your application.'

I laughed a little. 'It's true,' I told him. 'I have been thinking about medical school, but I have been praying about it and waiting for a sign from God.'

He looked at me, without judgement or surprise, and said, 'OK, well the Dean of the medical school asked me to come and find you. I will tell the Dean what you are saying.' He turned around to leave and then turned back. 'Do you have any idea when you will know?' he asked.

I shrugged. 'I don't. I'm sorry,' I said.

A look of confusion spread across his face. 'So, what shall I tell the Dean?'

'Just tell him that I am praying about it and hopefully I will know soon.'

'OK,' he said and left.

I went back to the same routine as before, praying and waiting for guidance. After another two weeks, the man returned. He seemed a little anxious.

'The Dean wanted to know whether you have heard from God yet?' he asked.

I laughed again. 'Maybe,' I replied.

'OK,' he said. 'I don't want to rush you, but if you think you might be interested, please write a personal statement for me. You know, some information about your life, your plans for the future and so on. Don't worry about filling in the application form or anything. We got all the information on you from the university. If you can do that, we can see about offering you a place.' I nodded. 'I guess I can do that,' I said.

He smiled. Then just like the last time, he turned to go, but this time, I called out to him. 'Excuse me,' I asked. 'But how did you find out where I was living?'

'I must admit it took some time,' he said. 'We were looking for quite a while.'

'But why did you bother?'

'Because we got good reports on you. You were in the top one per cent of your class, so we thought you would be an ideal student.'

I thanked him, and he left. After he went, my aunty approached me, shaking her head in disbelief.

'I have never heard of a university or medical school doing anything like this in my life,' she said.

I nodded. It had certainly been unexpected.

'Now, you have your sign,' my aunt told me.

Velma's parents, Claudius, and Isabella Major in 1992 USA

Grandma Isabella and grandchildren in 1989

It's all About Grace

Grandma Isabella and grandchildren in 1989

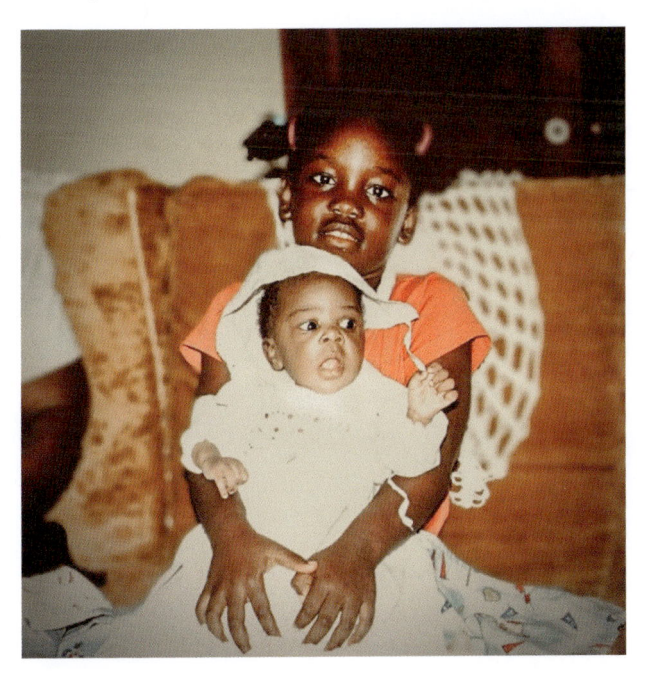

Grace with her younger sister in 1988

Chapter 3:
A Country Divided

As with many things in my life even before I had my "Encounter with God", faith had been the fulcrum of my life. Therefore, a few weeks after starting medical school, I made it a priority to find and connect with people who also had similar faith. After I discovered there was no Christian Fellowship at the School, I decided to put up an announcement on the student's bulletin board, inviting people to a meeting. It said:

> *'If You are a Christian, you are invited to a meeting in the Lounge at the Student's Dormitory, near the Beach on Friday at 7:30 PM for a time of Fellowship and prayer. Refreshments provided.*
>
> *Signed: Velma Major. (First Year)'*

I only expected a few students to turn out since I didn't know who the Christians were in the other classes, so you can understand my surprise when 15-20 students showed up. Most of them were from other African countries Nigeria, Angola, Sierra Leone, Zimbabwe, South Africa, and of course, Liberia; a truly international group of Christian students. This meeting heralded the formation of the Fellowship of Christian Medical Students at the A.M. Dogliotti College of Medicine, University of Liberia in 1975.

A year later, David Troko (who later became my husband) entered the Medical School and joined the Fellowship and we met and became co-leaders of the Fellowship and good friends and blossomed over the next four years.

The year 1979 was interesting in so many ways. On a personal level, my life had a real sense of direction. God had shown me what I was to do as my career. I was 25 years old, about to finish medical school and looking forward to getting married to my fiancé, David, who was also training to be a doctor.

Liberia's president at the time was a Baptist minister, (Reverend) William R. Tolbert Jr, whom my father supported as a candidate of his party (the True Whig Party).

President Tolbert had succeeded President William V. S. Tubman, who had steered Liberia's ship for an impressive 27 years, spanning 1944 to 1971. Much of this time, Tolbert had served as Tubman's deputy. After he became president, Tolbert introduced policies to bring development to the whole country and made efforts to redress inequalities in Liberian society economically, educationally, and politically.

Established in 1821, Liberia emerged as a haven for emancipated individuals of colour from the United States, an initiative steered by the American Colonization Society. When Liberia asserted its independence in 1847, the first African nation to do so, the country's first president had been a free-born African American.

However, as the nation grew, there were tensions between those who were descendants of immigrants and those who were descendants of Indigenous tribal groups. Despite that, a lot of intermarriages took place, but there were inequalities as with any mixed cultures and peoples.

In our family, we were somewhat protected from this issue since our ancestors came from both sides. Yet, we were always mindful of it. It felt like a deep divide in the heart of our country, a fracture that could either be mended or, as time passed, worsen, and split apart completely.

If that happened, it could tear Liberia to pieces. None of us could predict back then, as we went about our daily routines of work, study, worship, and community activities, that something catastrophic was on the horizon.

With the emergence of independent nations in Southern Africa and the tensions between communism and democracy, socialism and capitalism, the influence of these forces had an effect in Liberia amongst the young intellectuals. Change was coming too slowly, and they wanted change very fast.

In early April 1979, the Liberian government proposed an increase in the subsidised price of rice from $22 per 100 lb bag to $26.

Rice was Liberia's staple crop, on which much of the population depended. Some was homegrown, and some was imported.

What unfolded was the infamous 'rice riots' on April 14th, 1979. This led to injuries, destruction, and sadly, loss of life. The country was thrown into turmoil, property damage rising to the millions of dollars, and worse, a growing distrust and fear of each other.

Things eventually settled down; more or less, but the divide in Liberia had grown wider. The protest had seriously weakened the Tolbert government.

Then, nearly a year after the rice riots, on April 12th, 1980, Tolbert and most of his cabinet members were killed. This happened through a coup led by Master Sergeant Samuel K. Doe, a non-commissioned officer of the Armed Forces of Liberia.

On the day of the coup d'état, 12th April 1980, I was on call as an intern in the emergency department at the John F Kennedy Hospital in Monrovia, the largest teaching hospital in Liberia. My fiancé, David, came to pick me up for work in one of the hospital cars. He knew that I wouldn't be able to get to work any other way because there was mayhem throughout the city and public transport was unsafe and erratic.

Breaking Point

When I heard the car horn blaring and opened the curtains, I was surprised but glad to see him emerge from the hospital-owned vehicle. 'They need everybody at the hospital right away,' he said, as I answered the door. I was ready to go and only had to grab my white doctor's coat and name badge.

'There's been a coup. The president's dead. There are bodies everywhere. The wounded and the dead are being brought in in large numbers.'

I spent the entire day of the coup working in the emergency department, where I treated the wounded and saw first-hand the effects of the darkest day in our country's history. In the back of my mind, something else became clear. My wedding to David had been planned for 26th April, just two weeks away, but I knew immediately that events in the country would supersede it - we would need to postpone the ceremony.

The subsequent weeks unfolded with a crescendo of disquietude. Samuel Doe, the self-declared President, put the country on lockdown, imposing curfews. The very fabric of our country had unravelled. As I suspect with the world's recent COVID pandemic experience, the new normal was unsettling. Our beloved nation was being run by children; literally – they were all very young men, boasting military training but little to no education or any shred of experience for governance.

They had absolutely no idea what they were doing. What's worse, soldiers became a normal sight on Monrovia's streets. They drove around in stolen vehicles – hijacked cars from owners, government-owned cars, taxis, anything they could get their hands on to move from point A to B at high speed, whether they could drive or not. There were no rules. Law and order were non-existent. They strutted around with an attitude of omnipotence like they owned the place. Sometimes, they would shout and fire their guns in the air to intimidate and terrorise the public. A general sense of instability and mayhem prevailed. People were sometimes killed by stray bullets or executed, and nothing would ever be done about it.

The harrowing truth settled in - a land once serene, and a beacon of hope and freedom for African nations, had metamorphosed into a realm of unrelenting turmoil and anarchy.

In those days, when the wind of change swept over the land, strange things started happening. Citizens who disagreed with the new president, those who didn't belong to certain groups, or sometimes for no reason at all, just vanished.

The tales of these disappearances swirled through the streets, like leaves caught in a whirlwind, telling of folks snatched from their homes or plucked from the sidewalks by soldiers, gone forever. Vendettas raged back and forth. They were crazy times. Times when it was so important to have faith.

Without the knowledge that God would protect us, it would have been easy to slip into despair. People found new faith in Jesus that sustained them, and there were many testimonies of miraculous protection and escapes from death. Some people lost faith when they experienced such death, destruction and inhumanity perpetrated by people they knew, and thought were Christians or considered good people. But I believe God was still working amongst us, and in our family, our faith grew stronger. His grace was evident, and I believe that it limited the extent of the destruction and the length of time the carnage lasted.

Doctors working in the hospitals were also subject to abuse, intimidation, terror and arrests by soldiers and their relatives and sympathisers.

We felt the danger brought by the new order like a prickling on the skin. My father and uncle had served the previous government in different capacities - one in the House of Representatives and the other in the Senate.

We knew they were marked as prey.

Sure enough, my uncle got caught in the snare and got locked away in the main prison along with many other government officials. However, my father was able to slip away like a shadow, cleverly eluding their grasp. It helped that our family had ties in another part of the country, about three hundred miles away, a place named Sinoe County. My father had been superintendent and a member of the House of Representative there and so he was well respected and knew many people, so it became a refuge for him.

But even in that hideaway, he wasn't completely shielded. Soldiers came to Greenville, the capital of Sinoe, looking for dissidents and those with a connection to the old regime.

They sent soldiers to arrest my father, but the soldiers respected him and took him to the police station to wait for one of the coup leader's instructions. When one of the coup leaders arrived, he then questioned my father.

'Why didn't you come to respect and honour us?' they asked. 'We are the leaders now.'

'I have nothing to do with you or your leadership,' my father replied.

They kept him for several hours, then let him go. Knowing he was in grave danger; my father immediately took himself away to the family farm in a very remote part of Sinoe.

This was in the days before the internet and mobile phones, and it was as if he disappeared altogether. There was no way to contact him, which was difficult for us back home in Monrovia.

We did not hear from Papa for quite some time, but they never found him again, and we knew it was because God was looking after him.

In July, when my rearranged wedding to David was about to take place, we all knew we wanted my father there. However, the country was still very much in lockdown, and the soldiers were so unpredictable that most people opted not to travel at all. Any journey was fraught with danger. Even a short road trip carried the potential of the vehicle being stopped and confiscated. The driver and passengers, of course, could simply 'disappear', as so many others already had.

Despite the dangers, two of my brothers, Zachary, and Burke, made the decision to embark on the 360-mile expedition to locate Papa.

They employed various modes of transportation, including walking far distances along the route and navigating treacherous dirt roads and terrains. Remarkably, after many hours and days of searching, they found Papa and brought him back to Monrovia without any further trouble.

This was a period when people disappeared after stepping out to the local store. Yet here was a government official, in hiding, being driven across the country. Once again, we thanked God for his love and protection.

The Wedding

David and I got married on 12th of July 1980. On our wedding day, amidst the turmoil consuming our nation, the ceremony seemed to bear even more weight. Our marriage was akin to making a bold statement: **We are one in Christ.**

Some of my ancestors were Americo-Liberians, while others hailed from indigenous roots. In contrast, David's family was wholly Indigenous. The occasion provided a pocket of serenity and rationality amidst the chaos. Even though the country was engulfed in a self-destructive war, much of it stemming from the cultural and economic divide between Indigenous Liberians and Americo-Liberians, the wider Cold War-influenced ideological movements in Africa of that time, our wedding showcased unity prevailing between these divisions amongst the people.

The government had 'decreed' curfews, meaning no one could leave their home after 6:00pm. Our solution? Get married in the morning.

We held our wedding at 10am in our local Methodist church, in a hall below street level. The curfew also extended to public gatherings, making it illegal to meet in large groups.

This also meant that to avoid suspicion, we didn't send out any invitations. Only our family and close friends were privy to our plans. Still, even with all the precautions we took, we defiantly danced with danger. We were aware that our joy could turn to sorrow if the authorities came, and someone was arrested or potentially worse.

In the grand tapestry of events, what transpired was a small, intimate wedding, a departure from the norms of the various Liberian traditions. But to us, it was perfect. A demonstration of our love, our Christian faith and most of all, our trust in God to protect us.

It's all About Grace

Left - Claudius Major Image: Velma's Father, escaped from the war in Liberia via Sierra Leone, 1990

Below - Velma and David Marriage, July 12th, 1980,

Chapter 4:
Our Marriage

It was 1982, two years after we were married, I got pregnant for the first time. Our families and friends were overjoyed as they were expecting us to get pregnant immediately after we married in 1980. One family member even wondered if David had 'sacrificed having children' to become a doctor. He only laughed at the thought! Absurd.

By Liberian norms, this constituted a lengthy period of childlessness at the start of our marriage. In fact, some of our friends and fellow Christians had become deeply concerned. They prayed for us in the hope we would one day receive the blessing of pregnancy.

'Do you think this is a form of sacrifice?' One well-meaning friend asked. 'That perhaps, because you invested so much time and effort in becoming doctors, you have somehow sacrificed the opportunity to have a child?' This is a very traditional, African way of looking at things, but by contrast, we were never worried and always believed it would happen when God decided the time was right. Honestly, we weren't trying.

We were getting to know each other by being married. Our steadfast faith in this belief was proven right when Grace was born in August 1983 at Phebe Hospital in Gbarnga where David and I were assigned to spend one year doing Rural Health Service for the Ministry of Health. Medical Doctors after training in our medical school did one-year compulsory service in a Rural Hospital or Clinic.

A year later, we had another child, a son called Aab Archibald – a name deliberately chosen, as with all our children - 'Aab', a Dan word for God, and Archibald, after my late older brother. By that time, my internship had wrapped up, and I had commenced my service at the ELWA (Eternal Love Winning Africa) Hospital, named after an SIM gospel radio station.

The hospital was started in the 50's by American missionaries located in a part of Monrovia called Paynesville.

Most of the doctors there came from abroad, North America and Europe, and I was the first Liberian doctor on the staff, having been recommended by a missionary doctor who taught at the medical school I attended.

When David finished his training, he also began to work there as a colleague as well as husband.

In 1985, five years after the coup that had turned Liberia upside down and resulted in a military dictatorship, elections were held. The country was supposed to be returning to civilian rule.

But the man who instigated the coup, Master Sergeant Samuel K Doe, was reluctant to relinquish power. He decided to declare himself a civilian, form a new political party called the 'National Democratic Party of Liberia' and run for president. Surprise, surprise – he won.

Of course, the elections were seen as fraudulent by most observers, and there was a national outcry. Little could be done, however. The head of the elections commission made a public statement that he had to accept the outcome, as otherwise, the country would be plunged into further war and chaos, which nobody wanted. Within a year of taking office, the new, civilian Doe government was riven with infighting.

Various members of the original coup vied for power, and one was executed after plotting to usurp Doe. It was clear to all of us that the country's political situation would not be improving anytime soon.

Just to prove the point, there was then another uprising, which attempted to overthrow the military government. Most of the original 17 who had overthrown the government in 1980 were killed. These continued problems in Liberia troubled us greatly.

They reflected not just on the nation but on the whole continent of Africa. Emerging from the dark times of colonialism and slavery, Liberia had always been seen as something of a trailblazer, an example to other African nations who also yearned for independence. It was as if Liberia was a statement to the world: 'Look! Black Africans can govern themselves. Here is the proof.' Now that the country lurched from one crisis to another, the power of that statement was being lost.

Physically, you can rebuild a town, but emotionally and mentally, you cannot repair the damage so easily.

The trauma remained within Liberians and still does today. People take two steps forward in reconciliation and healing then three steps backwards. They return to familiar patterns, back to their tribal affiliations and the divide remains.

I alone know the plans I have for you, plans to bring you prosperity and not disaster, plans to bring about the future you hope for...

- Jeremiah 29:11

Our Marriage

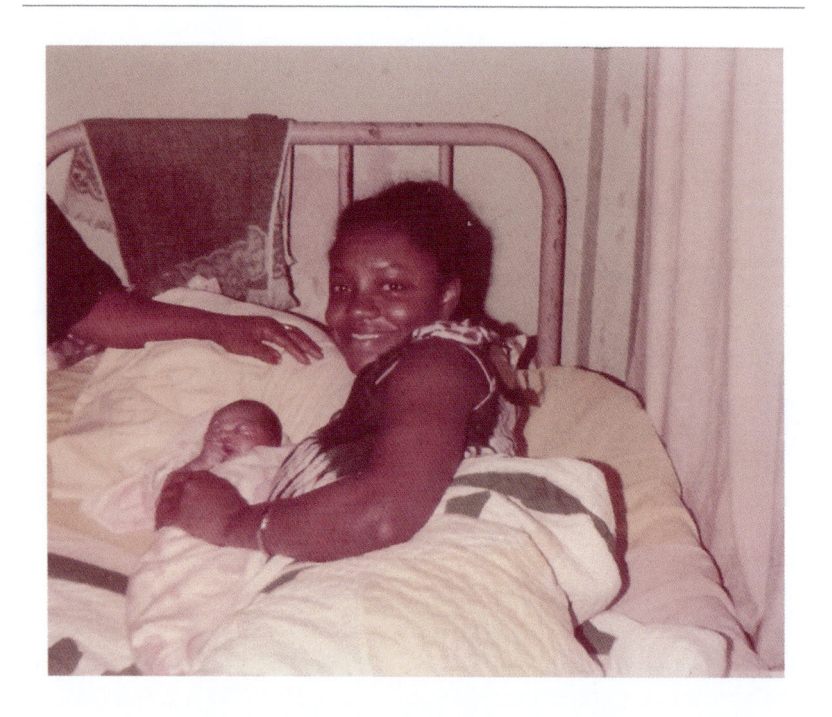

Above: Grace, only a day old with Mama Velma in Phebe Hospital, August 1983

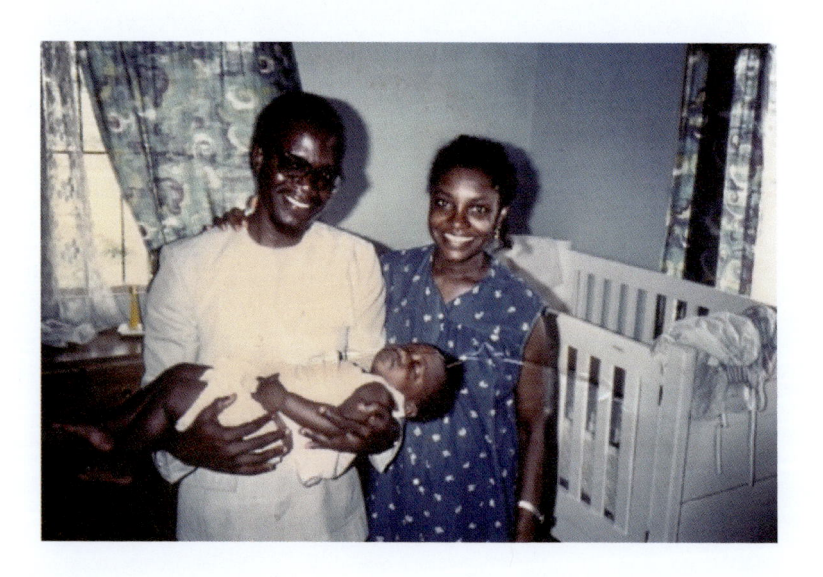

It's all About Grace

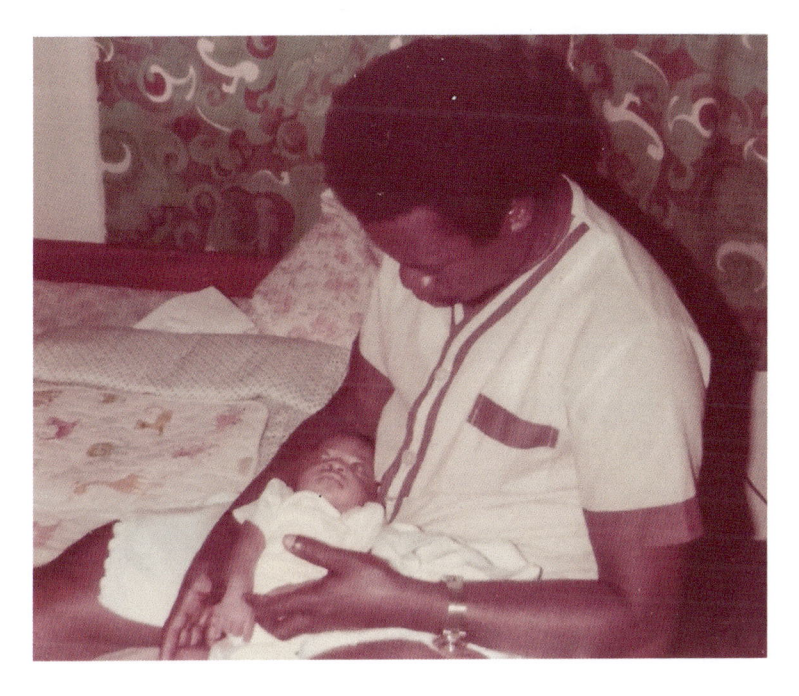

Above: Baby Grace , a few days old with Daddy David, 1983

Below: David and Velma with Grace a few months old with some Missionary Friends, The Robertsons, at Phebe Hospital, 1983

Chapter 5:
Coincidences?

Amidst all of this, at the end of 1985, a paediatric neurologist called Dr Eric Zurbrugg from Chicago came to work with us at ELWA. He was, like most visiting American doctors, a committed Christian, so David and I invited Eric, who everybody called Rick, and his wife Jo, who was also a doctor, for a meal at our house. By then, Grace was two years old, and her brother, Archibald, was one. Dr Zurbrugg was enchanted by the children and made a short video of them on a camcorder.

He was especially taken with Grace, who was running around and talking happily. She was such a lively child. We all enjoyed watching the video back, and it helped cement in our minds how blessed David and I were. Liberia may have been trapped in a vice of hardships, but within our walls, within our family, by God's grace, something beautiful blossomed.

In February 1986, David and I decided to travel to the USA to prepare for the FMGEMS (Foreign Medical Graduates Examinations in Medical Sciences); pre-qualification medical exams for foreign medical graduates to study and work in the USA. We chose Chicago because of our connections with Dr. Dave Van Reken who had worked with us in Liberia and been our teacher in medical school.

We left Grace and Archibald with some friends who could look after them while we were away and stayed with a lovely family in Chicago that Dr van Reken introduced us to. They were incredibly kind. We did not have to pay rent, and we did not have to buy our own food. They even helped us to organise a car to get to and from Kaplan International where we went daily to study for our exams.

Every Sunday, we attended the local church, where we would see Dr van Reken's extended family who also went to the same church. Just like us, they were a family of doctors and Christians. Even though we were from different parts of the world, we had a great deal in common.

Coincidences?

Just before we left America, in August, the church held a get-together to say goodbye to us, which was a lovely gesture. We had been active in their church community while we were there, singing in the music group and taking part in other activities, so we appreciated them taking the time to acknowledge our departure.

At the farewell party, Dr. Van Reken told us he would be returning to Liberia for a research project concerning malnourished children. He asked if he could stay with us while he was conducting this work, and of course, I said yes.

At the time, I did not give this much thought. It was only later, when I was on the plane home, that it crossed my mind that this request was a little strange.

As Dr. David van Reken worked for the same missionary organisation we did, he would be entitled to stay at the mission guest house on the hospital campus. He also had in-laws who lived there and could potentially stay with them. The bottom line was that he did not need to organise his own accommodation. I guessed that he simply enjoyed our company and gave it no further thought.

Roughly three to four weeks down the line, back in Monrovia, I got a call saying Dr. van Reken had touched down. One of the mission's drivers was set to pick him up from the airport. So, I hurried over to the guest room, rearranged things and changed the bedsheets to make everything ready for his arrival. He arrived at about 10 o'clock in the evening, and I welcomed him with a cup of tea and a sandwich.

Dr van Reken stayed with us for two weeks joining in easily with our family. Every morning, he would get up, make himself a packed lunch, go to the hospital to conduct his project, then return to our house in the evening. Usually, we all ate dinner together and treated him as if he were a part of the family.

Earthquake!

One night in the middle of his stay, Dr van Reken arrived back at our home late and went straight to bed. David was on call at the hospital, and I was at home with the children, so I put them to bed then also went to bed myself. It was a completely ordinary evening in our house, but that was about to change.

I sat on my bed, reading a book when I heard Grace crying, followed by footsteps. She came running to me in my bedroom.

'Mummy!' she cried, 'Mummy! My head, my head, my head!'

'Grace,' I replied, 'what's the matter?'

I felt her head. She did not seem to have a fever, which was puzzling. In Liberia, a tropical country, one of the first things you think of when someone complains of a headache is the possibility of malaria. However, malaria is usually indicated by the presence of elevated temperature.

Regardless, for the time being, I worked on the basis that malaria was the most likely possibility, even though we took sensible precautions.

Like most Liberians, we had screens over the windows and doors, and every Sunday, the whole family took a malaria prophylaxis to prevent infection. As you might expect in a family in which both parents were doctors, we took preventative medicine very seriously.

I sat Grace on the bed next to me and soothed her for a while. I asked if she had fallen or bumped her head.

She told me that she had not. It seemed my voice and presence calmed her, and after a time, she began to doze off by my side. Eager to provide my little girl with some pain relief, I phoned David at work.

'Everything OK?' he asked.

'I think so,' I told him. 'But Grace has woken up with a headache. When you come home from work, can you bring some Calpol for her, please?'

'Sure,' David replied. 'I'll be home soon.'

At that stage, we were both concerned. Small children don't usually have headaches. Grace was a very healthy three-year-old who had hardly ever been ill. I thought perhaps Grace had fallen from the climbing frame in the garden or run into a wall, but the childminder assured me there had been no accidents at all.

When David returned home, we gave her some Calpol then sat together on the bed, all three of us. David and I discussed the situation, trying to come to a mutual conclusion as to why our three-year-old should be suffering from a headache bad enough to wake her up. As we were talking, with Grace between us on the bed, she began to have a fit.

Her little body went into convulsions, her limbs and her shoulders jerking up and down. It seemed particularly bad down the right side, and her eye on that side turned inward too. Obviously, it was horrifying for both of us.

Even though we were medically trained, the shock of seeing our small daughter convulse in that way was incredibly alarming. We looked into each other's eyes and hoped it would soon end. Fortunately, it did not last very long. The spasms died down, and as the fit abated, Grace lay very still on the bed, as if the episode had drained a great deal of her energy.

Thanks to the grace of God, it immediately occurred to me that we had one of America's leading paediatricians asleep in our guest room.

Surely Dr van Reken would be able to recommend a course of action to us. I went to wake him and told him what was going on. He immediately came to look at Grace, and I could see from his face that the situation concerned him.

'What do you think is happening?' I asked.

'In truth, I don't know,' he said.

Between Dr van Reken, David and myself, the discussion resumed about Grace's affliction. We talked about our family history and conditions that relatives may have had, but nothing seemed to equate to what we were seeing.

We had three doctors there who, between them, had specialisms in tropical illnesses and childhood disorders, and yet, our combined knowledge could not provide an answer. It was clear that Grace would need to go to hospital.

We took her into ELWA in our car, and that night, we made a circle of prayer around her hospital bed, asking God to give wisdom so that we might get to the root of the problem and hold in place whatever was causing her illness.

One by one, we ticked off the possibilities. Initial examination failed to show up anything significant. Blood tests confirmed Grace did not have malaria. Her haemoglobin levels were excellent.

The doctor tried to check for meningitis too, but Grace did not cooperate, which made the test difficult to administer. That was the one obvious possibility we were unable to rule out.

While in the emergency room, she then had a couple more seizures. It was rapidly dawning on all of us, that *this* could be quite a serious situation.

Dr van Reken, David and I continued to discuss. We knew, of course, that the type of fit she was suffering, known as a 'focal seizure', was not associated with epilepsy but rather with something pressing on her brain, a kind of mass, or an infection. She was given a broad-spectrum antibiotic for 10 days and treated with antimalarials. And to reiterate, there were no recent accidents or bumps on the head that could explain all of this.

The confusion we felt was compounded by the fact that Grace had always been such a healthy child. From a medical perspective, everything about her had been close to perfect.

Her weight at birth was over the 95th percentile, and she had maintained that sort of level ever since. All the necessary vaccines had been administered at the correct times, as you would expect of a child born to two doctors.

She was playful, happy, and curious. People were always delighted by her, and throughout the first three years of her life, every single developmental milestone had been met with time to spare.

She was attending nursery and doing extremely well. She loved to read. Most strikingly of all, until she had the first seizure that night, Grace had been ill barely once with a childhood viral infection called 'roseola infantum', which gave her a fever that lasted for 24 hours, followed by a rash. Once that cleared, she was completely fine, and this history of optimal childhood health made the crisis she now faced even more worrying.

While waiting for news from the blood tests, in the emergency room, it happened again. Grace suffered yet another fit.

As it abated and my beautiful little girl slowly regained consciousness, we realised this one was different.

She had become paralysed down one side of her body. Terror whipped through me like an electric shock. *What on earth was going on?*

My mind turned back to the comments we received before Grace was born. People wondering if we had made a kind of sacrifice, by devoting so much time to our studies. Now I thought of other scriptural parallels. What was God wanting to teach us in this situation? Did He give Grace to us and then allow this to happen? A well-meaning relative did ask me the question, as if we were being tested. But we did not believe that this was what God had planned for our daughter, but I cannot deny that the thought flashed across my mind.

I feared that Grace may have suffered a form of stroke or something else to impact one of the hemispheres of her brain. The doctors examined her again and assured me her brain was working. Like David and I, they could tell something was wrong but were unable to specify.

By this point, it was 1 a.m., and Grace was stable. David and Dr van Reken returned to our house, while I settled myself in to stay the night with Grace in the hospital. I didn't really sleep much.

By morning, after a night full of prayers, Grace seemed to be doing much better. The paralysis she had experienced was gone, and she could move all her limbs and talk again. What a mighty God we serve!

'Mama,' she said, 'my head hurts.'

I took her temperature and discovered she now had the beginnings of a fever. It was a relief that the awful symptoms of the previous evening had receded, but it was also clear we were not out of the woods, not by a long way. Whatever was going on in Grace's brain was manifesting itself through a variety of symptoms, and we needed to find the underlying cause of it, fast.

Before we took Grace to the hospital, David and I made a circle of prayer around kneeling on our bed and asking God for her life and for wisdom. Grace was discharged from hospital that morning after the results came back from the lab. Back at home, she continued to complain of the headache.

Coincidences?

Perplexed, Dr van Reken suggested we write to the American paediatric neurologist, Rick Zurbrugg, who had spent a month at ELWA Hospital working with us the year before, visited our home and filmed Grace on his camcorder. This seemed a sensible idea. We all realised we had reached the limits of medical technology available in Liberia at that time. We could not do CAT scans or MRI investigations. There was no neurologist in the country for consultation. With all of us at a loss to explain Grace's symptoms, some specialist input was clearly required.

'Yes, let's ask him for his opinion,' my husband said. 'Maybe he can suggest something. It has to be worth a try.'

Dr. van Reken was returning to the USA. He was due to leave the next week. Our plan was to send the letter now and then call Rick when he got there.

In the meantime, we'd keep Grace on antibiotics and do our best to manage the situation. Coincidentally, a friend of ours was also going to America, a week before Dr. van Reken.

This was right when we brought Grace back home from the hospital, so David handed her the letter to mail once she reached the US. That way, it would get there faster than if we sent it from Liberia.

When Dr van Reken left, he told me he would investigate the matter as soon as he arrived back in America.

'Velma,' he said, 'try not to worry. We will see what we can do.'

'...Even if I go through the deepest darkness, I will not be afraid, Lord, for you are with me.'

- Psalm 23

Divine Intervention

After Dr van Reken departed from Liberia, a letter from Rick Zurbrugg arrived for him in Liberia. It was collected by the mission post office, who gave to his aunt in law to send to him via a missionary returning to the USA the next week.

Due to her quick thinking, she noticed the sender was Dr. Zurbrugg with a Chicago address and asked Dr. Van Reken's research partner about it. He encouraged her to open the letter and check whether there was anything concerning the management of care for Grace. And yes, it was 'all about Grace'. It said:

> *Dear David and Velma,*
>
> *I remember Grace, David, and Velma's daughter. It could be a brain tumour. Tell David and Velma to bring her at once. We will do what we can. Tell them not to worry about the money. Just come as soon as possible.*
>
> *With my very best wishes,*
>
> *Dr Rick Zurbrugg*

I found myself again wondering how this could be possible. My only explanation was that God's guiding hand was controlling the situation. Although we were well paid by Liberian standards, David earned $500, and I only earned around $250 per month.

We had no American medical insurance, and the costs of such a trip, even without any medical bills, would be well beyond our means. Dr Zurbrugg's generosity again demonstrated the twin power of prayer and Christian fellowship. Through God, these things became possible.

Beneath our gratitude and appreciation for Dr Zurbrugg's offer lay a level of curiosity. The letter did not say how Grace's treatment in America would be paid for, simply that we did not need to worry about the money.

Was it going to be covered by somebody else? Would the hospital simply treat Grace without charge?

We had no idea what Rick had in mind, and of course, a small element of anxiety remained.

Like most people, we were aware that costs of medical procedures in the US could run to tens of thousands or even hundreds of thousands of dollars, especially for serious conditions.

The way most Americans negotiated this was through health insurance, but even then, you still heard horror stories of people whose insurance claims were refused, leaving them facing bankruptcy after their treatment.

We knew that Rick did not own a hospital, so the whole thing appeared quite mysterious. Beyond any of that, however, lay the knowledge that he was a doctor like we were and a Christian like we were.

We also knew that we had the prayers, support and backing of lots of Christians, both at home in Liberia and in America. In this way, we relied on our faith. We knew that this situation was not only down to Rick Zurbrugg or, for that matter, Dr van Reken or even us.

It was down to God. Our belief that God was guiding us would keep us strong through moments of doubt and fear. We had asked God for help through prayer, and He would help us in all sorts of ways that surpass the limits of human imagination.

It's all About Grace

Drs Jo and Eric Zurbrugg, who facilitated Grace's treatment in 1986, with their children from Chicago, 1984

Dr Douglas Anderson, Neurosurgeon in Chicago in 1986, performed the surgery without charge.

Chapter 6:
Miracle(s)

We made the bookings to travel to America as quickly as possible. To do so, it was necessary to obtain a visa from the American embassy, but because we had recently come back from the States, we still had multiple entry visas stamped in our passports. Grace, of course, didn't have these. Fortunately, the people working at the American embassy knew ELWA Hospital, and as many of the staff working there were American missionaries, they were on good terms with them. This helped to speed up our application.

Two days before we were due to leave, I received a phone call from one of the missionaries. 'Velma,' she said, 'we've been praying about Grace's situation every day, and I believe that God wants us to give you some money.'

I did not know what to say.

'It's only $1,000,' she went on. 'But we hope it will help to cover some of your expenses.

My father died six months ago, and I have received some inheritance. I have been waiting for a while, and the money just arrived this morning, so I think God intends me to give some of it to you.'

I thanked her for her kindness. My parents were able to give us some help, so by the time we flew to Chicago, we had $2,500 with us. In normal circumstances, which would have felt like a great deal of money, but we knew we had a lot of expenses ahead of us. I later learned that $2,500 was enough to pay for half a day in an American intensive care unit.

Before travelling to the airport, we held another circle of prayer over Grace. We just asked God to stabilise whatever was in Grace's head long enough that I could get her to America to receive the necessary treatment.

'Please God,' we asked. 'Just hold this problem in one place. *Don't let it go anywhere else.*'

We asked God to watch over her and prevent any further convulsions or fever until we arrived. The *worst* thing that could happen would be for a major complication to occur during the flight.

My mother moved to our house on the ELWA campus to help David look after our son, a toddler at the time, and my two nieces, who were living with us during that time.

The flight was problem free, so Grace and I arrived at O'Hare International Airport well rested and full of anticipation for what was to come. John and Elaine Stob's family, whom David and I had stayed with before, kindly offered their hospitality again, and they came to pick us up.

Fear and Hope

Dr Zurbrugg had left instructions for us to notify him once we had arrived in Chicago. For an accurate diagnosis, Grace needed a CAT scan as soon as possible and he had organised this on our behalf.

He had also arranged with a neurosurgeon to be on standby in the event his services were required. Once we arrived at the house, we called Rick, and he advised us to go to the hospital he worked at immediately. Once again, the thing that connected all these people was our shared faith in God. Our Chicago hosts and the doctors who would give their time to help Grace had all come together through faith. This is the true love of Jesus Christ connecting us.

Rick met us at the hospital, and he and I sat together as the CAT scan was performed. We watched the results appear on the screen, and both immediately gasped at what we saw.

'Have you *ever* seen anything like this before?' he asked.

'Never,' I replied. 'I have only seen pictures in a medical book. We don't have this kind of equipment in Liberia.'

It appeared that whatever was in Grace's head had pushed her brain to one side.

'What is this that we're looking at? Let's wait for the radiologist to come, and then we can discuss.'

The radiologist was called in immediately and took one look at the scan results and said, 'It's an abscess.'

'Abscess?' I asked. 'What is an abscess doing in the brain of *my* three-year-old child?'

The radiologist and Rick both sighed. 'Do you see these kinds of things in Africa?' Rick asked.

'No,' I replied. 'And even if they were there, we wouldn't know. We treat things empirically, based on other diagnoses. We wouldn't be able to detect this.'

'OK,' Rick said. He was very calm. 'We're going to call the neurosurgeon now and let him know what's happening.'

When Rick phoned the neurosurgeon, Douglas Anderson, he was informed that he had just gone home after completing his shift at the hospital. So, Rick, Grace and I went to Dr Anderson's house and took the CAT scan printout with us. The surgeon looked at it and asked the same question.

'Have you often seen things like this in Africa?'

I gave the same answer I gave to Rick: 'No.' He shook his head.

'Well, neither have I,' he said. 'I have never seen an abscess like this. It's the size of a small grapefruit.'

Of course, I was taken aback. That's a huge growth inside the head of such a small child. Only a month had passed since her first seizure, and the abscess was that large. If we had not been able to bring her to the US, the consequences could have been awful. Even now that we were there, it was obvious something had to be done very quickly.

'The problem,' the neurosurgeon said, 'is that a growth of this size, which has been there for a month requires immediate action. We cannot sit on it. The longer we wait, the more chance that the abscess could rupture and create further complications. But I am extremely busy for the next week or so.'

My heart sank a little. Another week of waiting. What might that mean for Grace?

'I have cases back-to-back for the next seven days. So, what I suggest,' he went on, 'is that we make a start on this tonight.'

'Thank you,' I replied. 'This is why we are here, and I am eternally grateful to you because I know you are not on call tonight, and this is something you are doing for the love of God.'

This man did not know us. There had been no conversations about money, and yet, only a few hours after our arrival in America, we were sent to the hospital where Doug worked, the Loyola University Medical Centre, in the south of Chicago. He called ahead to make all the arrangements and to let the Neurosurgical Resident that was on call know we would be coming. Once we were admitted and all the lab work was completed, they would call Doug, who would then join us, to perform the surgery that very night.

Our host family drove us to the hospital, and I went in with Grace. Before long, Doug arrived, and Grace was taken in for surgery. Everything was a blur. I waited in the lobby, where I prayed and paced up and down. It took slightly over an hour before Doug reappeared, and it was a heavy moment as I stood face to face with him. If it was bad news, it could be the *very worst* kind of bad news.

'Yes, Velma,' he said. 'It was an abscess. We drained it and have managed to remove about ten millilitres of pus.

We are hoping that will be enough, and we have placed a suction drain on the site of the abscess for now to continue the extraction process.

Anyway, she is conscious again now. She's crying and moving all her limbs.'

'Oh, thank God!' I said.

This was hugely important news. Any operation on the brain has the potential to lead to a stroke or other major complications. The fact that Grace had regained full mobility suggested that pitfall had been avoided.

'And she's asking for you.' Doug smiled as he spoke.

So, Doug took me up to the intensive care unit. Grace was drowsy and soon fell asleep, as she had been given medication. She had a huge bandage around her head, which was effectively holding her head together.

'Tomorrow, we'll do another CAT scan,' he told me.

From there, that hospital became home. We stayed there for five weeks – a long and trying time.

While back in America, I reconnected with the church group I had befriended on my last visit.

They were so incredibly supportive, and some of them began to come to the hospital with me.

Once again, the power of all that collective prayer gave me so much strength. I was sure it would keep Grace safe.

Nonetheless, there were a few twists and turns on the way. A type of bacteria was discovered around the abscess, for example, meaning Grace had to be given a specific kind of antibiotic. It was believed that this bacterium, called staphylococcus, was the cause of the whole problem, and we racked our brains to understand how Grace could have ever come into contact with it. How did such a problematic bacteria end up in Grace's brain?

The only thing I could think of was that about a month before she had her first seizure, I had noticed a small boil on her bottom when bathing her. I had taken her to the hospital I worked, where a colleague of mine made a small incision and drained the boil. We gave her some antibiotics and thought that would be the end of it, but it seemed in retrospect, that the bacteria had somehow found its way into her bloodstream, and eventually her brain.

In the second week, another scan was undertaken, which showed that a large part of the abscess was still there.

A meeting of the doctors was called.

They were clearly concerned that the operation had not been as successful as they hoped.

'We need to go back in,' Doug said, finally.

The second surgery took six hours and was even more nerve-wracking than the first. After it was completed, Doug seemed tired and slightly stressed.

'That was difficult,' he explained. 'We tried to get as much out as we could, but the bleeding was too much, and we didn't want to cause more harm than good. So, we left some of the material in there. We will keep her on the antibiotics and see what happens.'

Naturally, this troubled me. I knew of the multiple complications that can arise from brain surgery from my own training and experience. At the back of my mind was always the fact that Grace was just three. This was a huge ordeal for such a young body to undergo, and a day or two after the second operation, she began to develop a fever. It was a confusing time. One day, as I stood in the hallway outside the ICU, I overheard the medical team discussing some of their fears.

'There's a risk of encephalitis,' one of them said.

'Definitely, something we need to be wary of,' replied another.

That was very worrying. I knew a colleague back home in Liberia whose two sons had both died because of encephalitis (inflammation of the brain). If that happened, I knew Grace would be in grave danger, even in Chicago with the best medical equipment and practitioners available. Around two weeks after the second operation, Doug consulted with me again. He told me their scans showed that no more fluid had been created, but the shell of the abscess remained on Grace's brain. He asked for my permission to make a final attempt to remove what was left of the abscess. If it remained, there was a chance of a relapse in the future.

I consulted with David over the phone, and we agreed that although Grace had already been through such an extended period of treatment, there was no point in falling short. So, I told Doug to go ahead and operate on Grace for the third time.

The final surgery went on for about three hours, and as with the previous two operations, I waited in the lobby and prayed for the entire duration. Some friends from Chicago came to join me, including the pastor from the church I attended while there. After the surgery, when Doug came into the room to find me, I was excited to see the whole surgical team with him. Everyone was smiling. It had to be good news!

'We are really pleased with what happened,' Doug said. 'We managed to get rid of nearly all the material. It wasn't easy. It was like an encasement, but we managed to shell it out.'

'Oh, thank God!' I cried.

'But I have an interesting thing to tell you.'

'What is that?' I asked.

'Last night, my mother called me, and she asked me if I had a patient called Grace Troko from Africa.' His mother lived in a place called South Holland, which was just outside of Chicago, and was a member of a prayer group there. 'News somehow reached her prayer group of Grace's case, and they had all been praying for us, without even knowing that it was her son doing the surgery!'

I laughed.

'Velma,' he went on, 'it seems like the *whole world* is praying for Grace.'

'Well, it does seem that way.'

'It is amazing how God works. Anyway, my wife is the daughter of a Lutheran priest in a part of Chicago called Oak Park. When you can leave the hospital, please bring Grace to our church.'

I could not thank Doug Anderson enough. From there, through continued prayer and trust in God, the situation stabilised. Grace was confined to hospital for more than a month in total, with intravenous tubes in her arms and legs, but all that was left of the abscess was a little scar tissue. The only thing we had to be concerned about was that it had been situated near what Doug referred to as her 'reading centre.' There was a chance, he said, that this could affect her development as she got older.

When we received the welcome news that Grace could be discharged, I went down to the finance office.

'OK,' they told me. 'This is your bill.'

I examined the piece of paper carefully. The three neurosurgical procedures that Doug had carried out were all free of charge. All the other consultants and professionals who had been involved had also worked for free, including anaesthesiologists, infectious disease specialists and consulting paediatricians and radiologists. However, the fee for the hospital bed, Grace's time in the ICU and an ambulance trip when she was sent for an X-ray at the veteran's hospital nearby still came to $40,000. I looked at the bill and raised my eyebrows.

'Oh, right,' I said.

'Do you have medical insurance?' the clerk asked.

'No, we have just come from Africa four weeks ago. No insurance.'

'So, what are you going to do?'

'I don't know,' I replied. 'I only have $2,500. Can I give you that for now and pay the rest in instalments over the next few years?'

The clerk turned to her manager behind her. 'Are you going to keep us here until we pay the money?' I asked.

'No, no,' she laughed. 'We can't do that.'

The manager said, 'Just pay what you can regularly until it is cleared.'

I thought it would take years. So, I said, 'Thank you very much', as we were discharged from the hospital that day.

Very soon after leaving the hospital, we took Doug up on his invitation and visited him and his wife at their church. The service took place on All Saints Day, during which Doug presented Grace to the church community.

On the same day, a lady member of the congregation was celebrating her 99th birthday, and it was such a beautiful moment, seeing two people, from completely different corners of the world and so different in age, brought together to celebrate lives lived through Jesus Christ.

Call to me when trouble comes; I will save you.

- Psalm 50:15

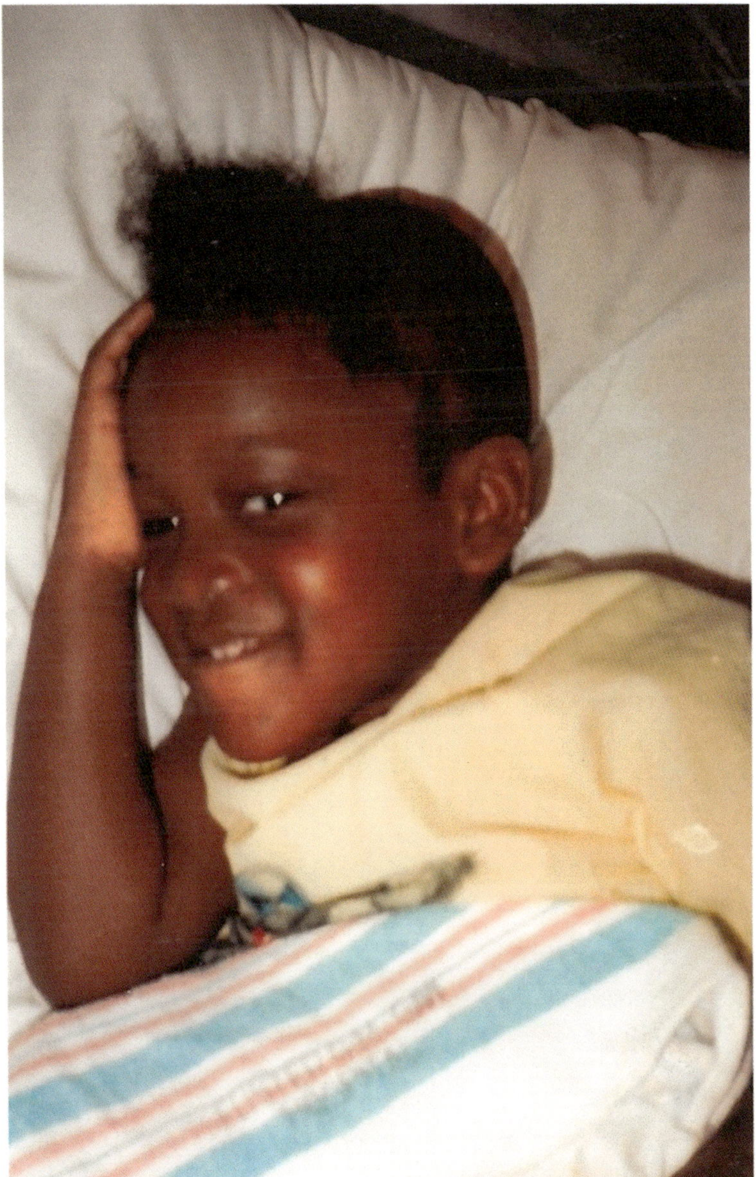

Loyola University Medical Centre Chicago, Illinois, 2022

Velma and Grace return to Loyola to meet Dr Anderson and say thank you, July 2022

It's all About Grace

Chapter 7:
A New Home

Within a week of the celebration at Doug's church, we returned to Liberia. Life returned to something like before. Grace's head had been shaven on one side, which gave her an unusual appearance and made the scar very visible, but this was a minor inconvenience compared to what we had all been through.

Grace kept asking what had happened to her hair. I told her the doctors had to shave it to get some bad things out of her head. Every month, we continued sending money to the hospital in Chicago. For us, it was a huge debt and took up all my salary, meaning we lived on David's alone. Some Christian friends of ours held a collection and sent us a little more financial help.

Still, it appeared this bill would be hanging over our heads for quite a long time. Over the course of the next year, we paid off around $14,000. In October, a week before Liberia's Thanksgiving Day, we received an unexpected letter from the Loyola University Medical Centre in Chicago.

Dear David and Velma,

We want you to know that we found it a privilege to help Grace in her hour of need, and we want to say thank you for your efforts in paying this bill. We know it must be very difficult for you.

We would also like to acknowledge your own work in healthcare. Like us, you are giving your time to care for the sick. After some consideration, the hospital has decided to cancel the rest of your bill.

It was yet another amazing piece of news and another example of God's love. How many pieces of fortune had we had along this journey? If Dr van Reken had never come to stay with us in the first place, none of this would have been possible. Since then, it had been series of miracles, progressively getting larger, culminating with the big miracle of Grace's full recovery. By then, the only thing that marked Grace out as different to any other child was that she needed to remain on anti-seizure medicine. Other than that, life was relatively normal.

Unfortunately, 'normal' during that period in Liberia also meant turbulence. The political situation of our homeland became ever more unsettled, and the country's political problems were not resolved. Over the next three years, things got worse and worse.

While our family grew with another daughter, Joy, born in March 1988, and our children got older, Grace started attending school and doing very well, with no reading problems at all.

Grace upon Grace

In late 1988, David went to the UK to do further training in surgery, through a special training programme. He would return to Liberia after a few months to start an orthopaedic specialist training at JFK Medical Centre in Monrovia.

In 1989, he was accepted on to another programme by a Christian orthopaedic surgeon in Merseyside, UK, which meant the whole family moving to England in February 1990. This year saw the beginning of Liberia's first civil war.

The timing of our move to England was another moment which was 'All About Grace', as the journey to the UK happened just at the outset of the war, initiated by the rebel invasion into south-eastern Liberia via Butuo. We travelled shortly after the invasion, but significantly, before it reached Monrovia.

We moved whilst I was heavily pregnant with Gayle. We were advised by two Christian friends for the whole family to leave together because we didn't know how the invasion would unfold.

Oftentimes, when Doctors from overseas come to the West, their families would remain in their home countries until they're settled.

We left most of our belongings behind, with only two suitcases and very little money. We didn't know where we would live or who we would be with for the next five years. Our first stop was Rainhill near Liverpool. David's first training job was in orthopaedics where he worked for two years with Mr Ben Bolton-Maggs a Christian surgeon in Liverpool. This was another 'grace' of God provision.

By the time we were settled in the UK, tragically, the events of the last decade or so had concluded in the tearing apart of our beloved home. Liberia's civil war was in full force. It started with a rebel invasion, which reached Monrovia, and the subsequent events turned into the darkest period of Liberian history. We followed the news from our new home in England with tears, anguish, despair, and broken hearts.

The timing of all this was not lost on us or those who knew us. A friend of ours, an old colleague from ELWA, wrote us a letter in which he said that it was as if God had picked us up and transported us from danger.

Our home city saw some truly awful tragedies. No one was safe. Monrovia became a centre for murder, mutilation, theft, and everything else. Our country had fallen apart. What's worse, members of our family and our friends were murdered, kidnapped, displaced in different countries around the world.

For us, it was so devastating to hear the stories. Our immediate family was and remains traumatised to this day from the war. David and I prayed for God to restore peace to our country, and we both resolved that when we were able, we would do whatever we could to help. It was clear to us that these sorts of acts would deeply wound Liberia's soul.

The whole population would be affected, and a generation of children would grow up grief stricken and traumatised. But God remained steadfast in his love and care for us. Our Christian family in the UK, loved, embraced, and truly cared for us during this time. To add insult to injury, in March 1994, my mother sadly passed away from a heart attack whilst in the USA. It was a really, *really* tough time for us, and it affected the whole family greatly.

Living by Grace

Grace , now 11 years old, started secondary school in September of that same year at Sutton Coldfield Grammar School for Girls.

After being in school for a few months, she had an *absence seizure* (one without convulsions) at school, which deeply frightened her. This was investigated at the local hospital where her dad worked. She was put on medication for two years and eventually, the seizures stopped. Other than that, we lived a happy family life in England.

Over the years, we hosted many international students from around the world, something I very much enjoyed. For me and my family, faith in God, through the Christian religion, was the thing that mattered most. We did not concern ourselves too much with all the various branches of Christianity and their different practices.

Other people may have called us evangelicals or charismatics, but we did not think like that. All these terms such as Baptist, Methodist, Episcopalian and so on did not matter.

What mattered was that we believed in Jesus, His word, His sacrificial work on the cross and His promises. Above all, we tried to follow what Jesus said as best as we can in loving others.

In this way, we were able to connect with other believers from all denominations of Christianity. Anglicans, Catholics, Orthodox – it did not matter to us. What mattered were our similarities, our shared beliefs, and values. Our differences were insignificant in comparison. To me, a Christian from Sweden or Australia is no different to a Christian from Liberia or anywhere else. If you follow Jesus, I consider you my brother or sister.

In 2003, after the Liberian civil war ended and the country began to stabilise, we began returning every year for a holiday, just to catch up with people and see old friends. It was good but also a little heart-breaking to go back. The country we had left behind was changed tremendously. While making these trips, David and I got involved with various local projects aimed at repairing some of the damage, both physical and psychological, caused by all the years of war.

In 2006, we were delighted when Liberia held free elections for the first time in many years, ultimately electing Africa's first female president, Ellen Johnson Sirleaf.

We attended the inauguration and participated enthusiastically in all the celebrations. It felt like a corner had been turned.

It's all About Grace

A New Home

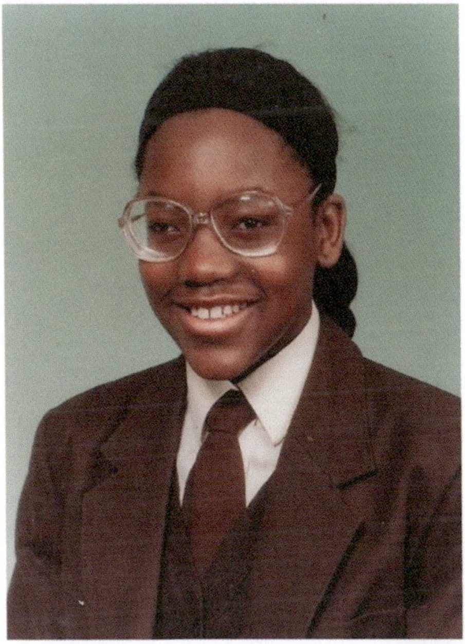

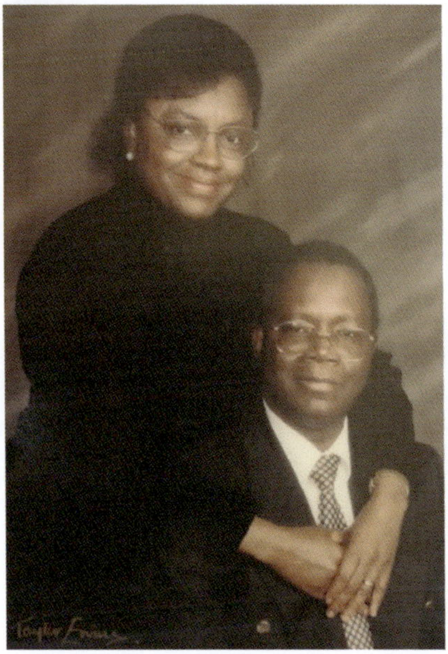

A New Home

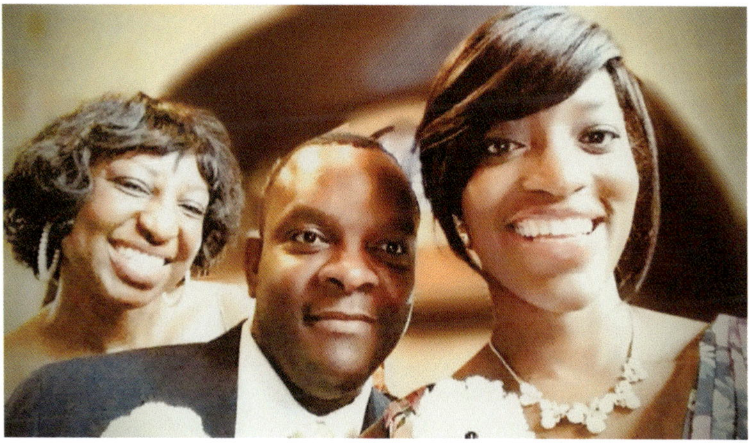

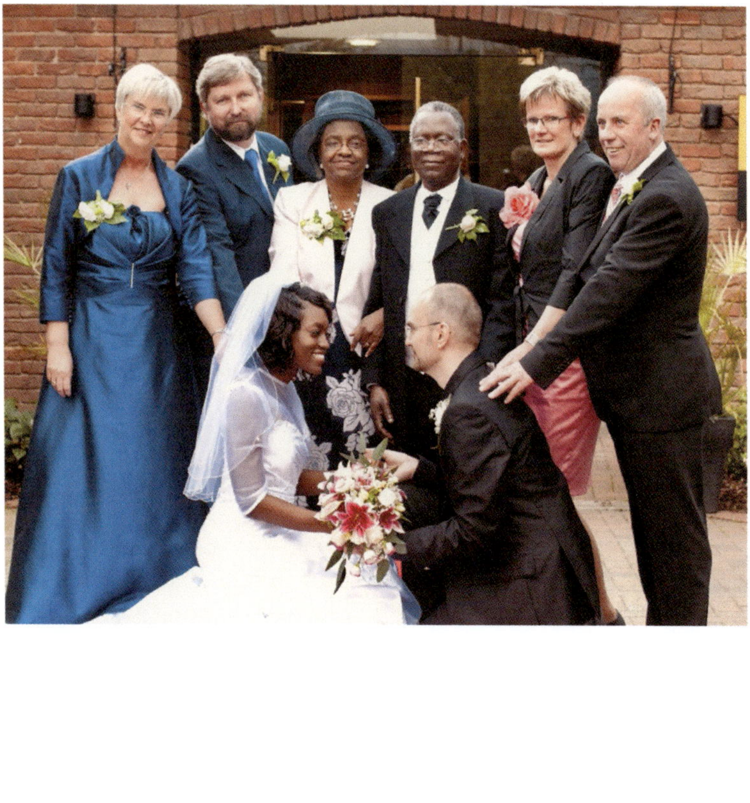

Epilogue

In 2011, David retired from working in the A&E Department of our local hospital after 21 years of service. Grace and Archi had completed university by then. In April 2012, we had our first family wedding in Sutton Coldfield.

Grace married Hagen, a German Christian whom she had met in South Africa in 2010. They were on the same DTS training course YWAM (Youth with A Mission), a Christian organisation in Port Elizabeth. It was a grand wedding with friends and family from all over the world joining. David was especially happy that despite all of Grace's health complications, he was able to walk his daughter down the aisle. After the wedding, David travelled to Monrovia to explore opportunities for returning to fulfil some of his long-held dreams for his home country.

In August 2012, David travelled to Liberia to firm up our plans to return and help the health service there. Where, specifically, would we direct our energy? Which projects would we prioritise? David did some voluntary work back at ELWA to get an idea of which areas were most in need.

Through some connections that we had in the medical world, David was then invited to attend a dinner hosted by the President of Liberia, Ellen Johnson Sirleaf, in honour of the American National Medical Association. It was a great honour. In a speech given by the President of the American National Medical Association, David received special recognition. At the end of the dinner, as Sirleaf was leaving, she stopped to where David and I were sitting and said:

'David, I want to thank you for all the work you have done for the people of our country and all the service you have given Liberia.'

They had a short conversation, and it made us both so proud that David's lifelong commitment to his profession should be recognised by the country's president. He was a special, humble man, and it was a truly special moment.

Epilogue

It was one of those moments that becomes even more special in retrospect.

On February 20th, 2013, just three months after being congratulated by the president, David was dead.

Several months prior, he had developed what seemed to be a seasonal cough, albeit a little irritating, just before he went to Liberia in August. Whilst in Liberia, he had received treatment for the cough, but ominously, it wasn't going away. Upon his return to the UK for Christmas in December 2012, he went to see his GP.

The news was **devastating**.

It seemed unbelievable, but my husband had lung cancer, at quite an advanced stage, and was completely unaware. David had always lived a healthy life, did not smoke, and drank very little alcohol. He exercised often and was sensible with what he ate.

There was no way to predict something like this. He began having chemotherapy back in England, but the treatment started much too late and could not halt the disease. He was just 66 years old when we buried him in Monrovia two months later, as he had requested.

David's death shattered the lives of our family. He had been my darling husband for more than 30 years, a wonderful father, a compassionate and committed doctor, and above all, an exemplary Christian.

Even today, it still affects us. We have never gotten over it.

I suppose we have made our peace with it and learned to accept it, but the pain of his loss will always be there. It is now over ten years since his passing, and I still think of him every day.

My children – Grace, Archibald, Joy, and Gayle – are all grown up now and living productive, happy lives. Grace lives with her husband in Germany, Archibald is married and lives with his wife in South Africa, Joy is married with two children and lives in Sutton Coldfield and Gayle also lives nearby.

Life and, most importantly, God has been good to us, and it is important to remember that, despite the tragedy of losing my home, and my husband, especially so early after retirement, it is still *'All About Grace'*. My greatest sadness was that David died before he could fulfil his dreams of returning to Liberia to help the country in its recovery.

I have tried to keep some of those ideas alive by developing a plan that we had for a village based around farming and community.

David bought some land for this purpose, and since his death, we helped to build a primary school there for the local people. We have now started a poultry farm and a vegetable garden to feed the children. Every three months, I send them a little money from England, and when I do so, I feel I am honouring my husband.

We call it the David Troko Eden project, a fitting legacy for a wonderful man.

As this book was being written, a new trip to America was planned. Grace and I returned in July 2022, to reunite with the wonderful doctors, Dr Douglas Anderson, the neurosurgeon, and Dr Eric Zurbrugg the paediatric neurologist, who used their expert skills to save my Grace's life and our fantastic friends in faith who gave us so much support.

We attended the event that was planned to honour the work of David and Ruth van Reken. It was an amazing experience to go there and see them again, and in a way, it brings my and Grace's story, full circle. As much as anything, it was very special for Grace, now an adult, to have the opportunity to personally thank the people who worked so hard to enact God's miracle.

Still, sometimes in my quiet moments, I wonder where I should be. As I get older, I often think of my country.

The last time I went to Liberia I found myself asking God for His guidance.

Epilogue

'What do I do, God?' I asked.

I received a very clear answer.

'Go back to England,' he said. 'Your children need you, and you will do great things from a distance. Stay there until I tell you to move.'

I had promised all those years ago to devote my life to Jesus, and so I listened. England for now remains my home, and it will be until God decides I should leave.

> '...For it is by God's grace that you have been saved through faith. It is not the result of your own efforts...'
>
> - *Ephesians 2:8-10*

Grateful

Grace and I would like to express our enormous gratitude to all the people who helped us, in Africa, America and the UK. Thank you to all our family members who supported us by prayers and finances and to the editors who have patiently worked with me in getting this book published.

While I know that God connected us and guided the miracle to happen, so many people, most of whom did not know us at all, offered their time and resources, completely selflessly. This was not only a demonstration of Christian fellowship, but an indication of the goodness in all their hearts.

Epilogue

It's all About Grace

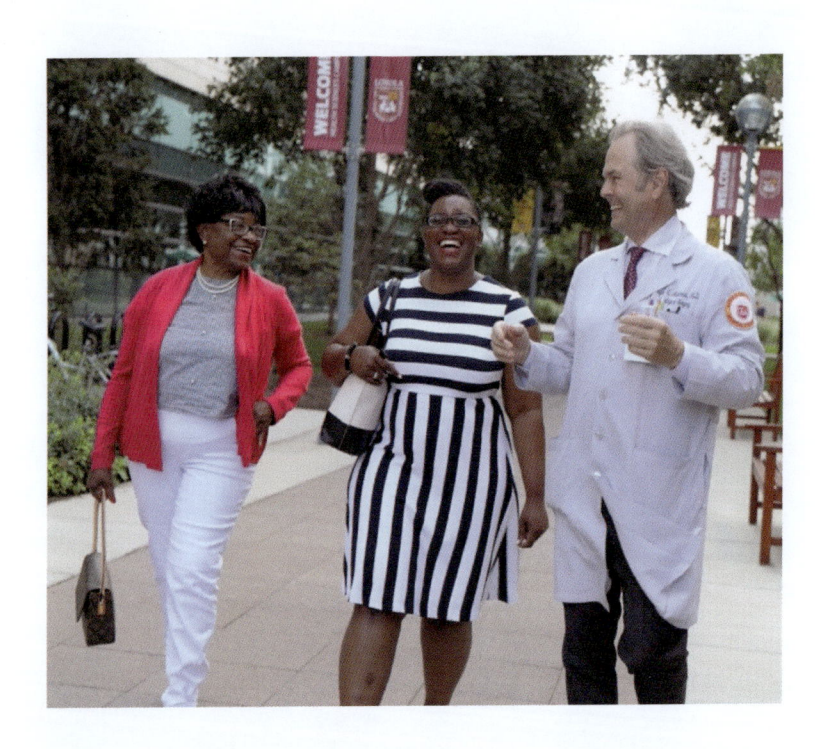

Epilogue

Printed in Great Britain
by Amazon